D1287726

A True Story of a Hero

CLAYTON SPARKS
Leaves His Mark

Written by
Abby Gray

Illustrated by
Dee Everett

Clayton Sparks Leaves His Mark

Written by Abby Gray

Illustrated by Dee Everett

Editors: Jean Sime, Brenda E. Cortez

Layout: Michael Nicloy

Hardcover ISBN: 979-8-9853960-2-7

Paperback ISBN: 979-8-9853960-3-4

Published by BC Books, LLC
Publisher: Brenda E. Cortez

BC BOOKS, LLC

Printed in the United States of America

love
inspire
be kind
have faith

Clayton Sparks was an incredible man who was kind from a very young age.

Clayton made friends wherever he went,
always smiling to brighten their days.

Clayton knew the importance
of helping others.

He made sure to pass
that message on.

He encouraged friends to share by saying,
"You can't take it with you when you're gone."

For his birthday, he asked for money to help those who were in need.

He took that money to a local food bank to
see how many people he could feed.

Clayton lay awake one night thinking of those less blessed at Christmas

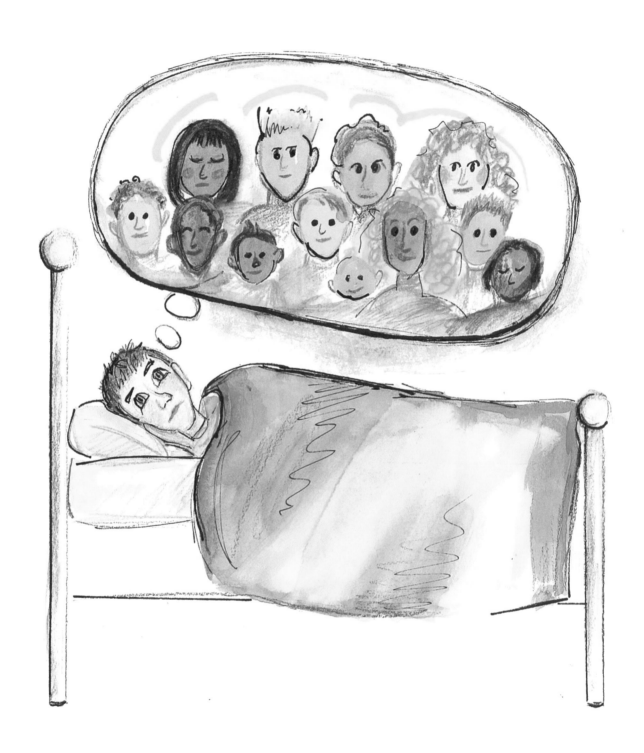

He asked for gifts from friends,
believing the joy of giving is within us.

Clayton sparked kindness in his friends as they gave gifts to many children.

By giving, they offered hope to others,
helping more than they envisioned.

One day Clayton went to be with the angels
but his mission was not yet through.

Because of his generous spirit,
he helped more than he ever knew.

Clayton's gift allowed a father of twins
to be there for every milestone and giggle

By choosing to share,
Clayton was a true blessing.
His generosity caused a big ripple.

Clayton's story lives on
through those he blessed.
He will always be an inspiration.

His kind, giving, soul touched so many lives,
even at his final celebration.

Clayton's love sparked hope for all.
He made the world a better place.

He left his mark on those he helped.
Through them, lives his
kindness and grace.

Activities to "Spark" Kindness

Children need some guidance on how to become empathic and start finding ways to reach out and give to others. Please use this list to discuss with your child ways your family can impact others.

Birthday Party Ideas:

▷ Have birthday guests bring money for a food bank to your child's birthday party. You can drive your child to the food bank and have him/her make the donation, or take the children to a discount grocery store and allow them to buy and deliver the food themselves.*

▷ Have guests bring almost-new items to your child's birthday party that they don't want and donate them to a women's shelter.

▷ Instead of having the birthday guests bring presents for your child, have them bring gifts for a child at a homeless shelter or foster home.

▷ Have the guests bring pet supplies (dog or cat food and pet toys) to your child's birthday party and donate them to a local animal shelter.

Holiday Activities:

▷ Find a school, group home or vocational center for children or adults with special needs, and buy Christmas presents for the residents that do not have families.*

▷ Ask your school counselor if there is a family that your family can help at Christmas.

▷ Contact a "soup kitchen" and see if you and your child can help prepare or serve meals, especially on Thanksgiving and Christmas.

▷ Make Valentine's cards for nursing home residents and have your child deliver them personally. Warm socks are also appreciated for residents.

▷ Get a group of children to visit a nursing home. Have them bring a Holiday activity or practice some songs to sing with the residents.

For Teens:

- Volunteer at a facility for teens and adults with intellectual and developmental disabilities.*
- When your child gets their learner's permit, remind them of Clayton's story, discuss organ donation and talk about the importance of becoming an organ donor.
- Volunteer as a coach or assistant coach for their favorite sport. Help children in the neighborhood with their homework.

Family Activities:

- Contact a non-profit to see what you can do to get your family or your child involved in an outreach program. Everyone benefits!

Most organizations would love for you to plan something for their residents; just contact them and see what your child can do to help! Please share your acts of kindness on social media with the hashtag #SparksKindness!

Clayton did these activities for the TLC Food Pantry in Willis, Texas, and Bridgewood Farms in Conroe, Texas.

Clayton Sparks was a real-life hero who grew up in Willis, Texas. From a young age, he encouraged others to be kind and inclusive. He made the world a better place by contributing where he could, and he was passionate about organ donation. In January 2019, Clayton was in a tragic skiing accident that took his life at the young age of 24. Clayton became an organ donor and blessed the lives of over 80 families with his corneas, tissue, and organs. The impact he made in this world, through both life and death, deserves to be honored. We hope this story will inspire children to make the world a better place, just like Clayton did!

Clayton was successful in business and had just earned his master's degree from the University of Houston. He was a great baseball player, often seen wearing a Hawaiian shirt, and a good friend to all who knew him. While we mourn the loss of Clayton, we honor him and keep his memory alive by sharing stories of how he inspired and helped others.

We encourage you to use this book as a conversation starter regarding organ donation with your friends and family. Please honor Clayton by registering to be an organ donor at registerme.org.
Partial proceeds from this book will go to the Clayton Sparks Memorial Foundation to continue the acts of service Clayton was so passionate about.

CLAYTON SPARKS MEMORIAL FOUNDATION

CPSIA information can be obtained
at www.ICGtesting.com
Printed in the USA
LVHW071045090223
738978LV00004B/106